Mildred Murphy, how does your garden grow?

Mildred Murphy, how does your garden grow?

by Phyllis Green

drawings by Jerry Pinkney

A Yearling Book

This book is dedicated
to the memory of my mother.

Published by
Dell Publishing Co., Inc.
1 Dag Hammarskjold Plaza
New York, New York 10017

Yearling ® TM 913705, Dell Publishing Co., Inc.

ISBN: 0-440-45590-1

Reprinted by arrangement with
Addison-Wesley Publishing Company, Inc.

Printed in the United States of America
First Yearling printing — March 1980
CW

Contents

❦

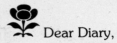 Dear Diary,

I'm Mildred. Mildred Murphy. I'm new here in San Rafael, California. I don't know anybody. We rent this big old green house till ours is built. It's going to be one of those modern things on sticks on a hillside. Actually it's almost on top of the hill and my dad bought a telescope so we can see the view for miles around. Fifteen miles maybe. We will be able to see Mt. Tamalpais one way and Novato the other way. I wish we could see New Jersey. I miss it so. I miss Allison and Jerry and Lynne. We played a lot. They didn't call me Mildred. Nobody called me Mildred in New Jersey. I was Mildew there. Boy, do I miss it. My mother says we need lonely times to think. I don't know if I like to think. Maybe when I'm thirty-eight I'll like it. Right now, I don't like to be one day without playing with someone.

I'm going into fifth grade when school starts but that's two months away. I guess I'll just shrivel up and die before that time comes with no one to play with. All the California kids live in new houses practically. Just old people live around here in old houses. We have three floors and a basement. We won't have a basement in the new house. Did you *ever hear* of that? Part of the house will be on a slab of cement and part of it will just be stuck over the hillside, built on air and sticks.

There is a girl, Josie McWhirter, one year older than I am, a block away but she's at camp for the summer. Then there are a couple of boys, six and seven years old, on the cul-de-sac but they're up in Jackson, Wyoming, for the summer. I don't think I care if they come back either because they would probably be pests. But how would I know? I haven't met them or Josie. I guess if somebody would call me Mildew again I wouldn't care what they were like.

Daddy put his telescope up on the third floor so he can look at stars. I was up there this morning looking at the neighborhood to see if I could find a friend. All I saw were people who had grown old with their houses. Some of them have even begun to look like their houses and property. Mrs. Murchison, next door, is quite chubby like her house with its bay window, and her hair is ragged and slightly sparse in places like her yard. I met her the first day here and what she said to me that I most remember was "The only growing things I bother with are people. Let the others have manicured lawns and prize begonias and fat tomatoes. My garden is people. I do volunteer work down at the Bureau for Runaway Teenagers. That's when I started to realize people need nourishing more than plants. I work one evening a week on the Suicide Prevention phone. On Sundays I visit the folks in the nursing home. Anybody can be an expert on Dutch Elm disease or dry rot, but how many know about the lonely souls that are dried up and withering away?"

Then she took my hand and said, "And you, Mildred Murphy, how does your garden grow?"

I looked up at Mrs. Murchison and didn't know how to answer.

"I don't know," I said. How can I help lonely souls? I'm one myself, now.

Mr. and Mrs. Johnson, on the other side of us, always dress in gray to match their house. Even their car is gray. And their maid wears a gray uniform, and she's so old I think she is faded gray though she must have once been black. She lives on the third floor. She is thin and sometimes she waves to me.

This morning she shook her finger at me as if to say "Don't you point that thing at me." meaning the telescope. I nodded my head and crossed my heart, meaning I wouldn't. Then she laughed. Real hard. She leaned back and laughed real hard. Her white teeth shone out of her grayness. We looked at each other across the way and laughed ourselves silly for about five minutes. I bet she would call me Mildew if she knew that was my name.

The only thing we have in the third floor is peeling wallpaper, the telescope and an old oriental rug Daddy lies on to study the stars. I wish my bedroom could be up there. But the ceiling slopes and I have a canopy bed. I wish I had a cot and I could live up there like a hermit which is what I must be anyhow.

Diary, let me tell you about the rest of the neighbor-

3 🌹

hood. Right across the street from us is a funny little skinny house painted yellow and only two stories high. A real nice old man lives there who spits tobacco. Also he wears a brown suit and never uses a handkerchief. He blows his nose by holding two fingers to it and shooting the snot on the ground. I tried it. It's kind of fun. But my mother saw me and said, "You know where the Kleenex are, don't you?" The man is Mr. Porter. Old Man Porter most of the people say. He bends when he walks. He never smiles at me when I go by his house but he always says, "Nice day."

It always *is* a nice day here. It's hard to get used to it. We haven't had a bit of rain and Old Man Porter says it won't rain till November. Then in the winter, it will rain but it won't snow. I really don't believe him. And he says his margarita daisies will bloom all year round. I don't think so.

There is a vacant lot next to Old Man Porter. Then a big white house that takes up a whole corner. It is the biggest house around. It has three stories too and a big porch that goes from the front of the house right around the side. It also has a garage, by the vacant lot. There is an unoccupied apartment above the garage. It has a dormer window and outside stairs that are partly covered by a bay tree. Bay trees grow in California, and if you want to know what they look like, think of a giant stalk of broccoli. The people that live in this white house are just about as old as my mother and father. They don't have children, but they had a mother who lived with them till last month when she died. Their names are Irene and Dan Calloway, and they both work, and Dan moves his chin in a strange way when he talks. On the weekends they grow roses all over their backyard and even in the side and front yards. Almost everywhere you look there are roses, and they are very happy for you to look at them and ask about them but very definitely you must not touch. Boy, did my parents lecture me on that. The Calloways are very polite and probably wouldn't say a word to me if I touched but would just get sick inside. Mr. and Mrs. Calloway are both blonde. They are sweet and sad looking. I think they are still crying over the mother that lived with them.

I forgot to tell you about Old Man Porter's lemon trees. He has two, on either side of his skinny yellow house and sometimes when I walk by instead of saying "Nice day," he'll say, "Nice day. Have a lemon." Then he'll scramble over, all bent up, to one of the lemon trees which look like big green bushes loaded with yellow pom-poms and break off a fat lemon for me to take home to Mom.

We have the weirdest bugs in our backyard. They're called potato bugs. They are swollen orange uglies. I wouldn't step on one for a million dollars. You could probably hear the squish all the way to New Jersey.

Somebody lives on the other side of Old Man Porter. I don't know who, but someone watches television all day in a bathrobe. I don't know if it's a man or woman. But with Dad's telescope I can see the television and the bathrobe. Whoever it is watches dumb shows.

5 🌹

That's all the people I've had a good look at so far. So, dear diary, you know where I live and what I'm doing. I will close you now and hide you in my underwear drawer and go down to the patio and practice blowing my nose into the grass.

Love, Mildred

When I woke up this morning I could hear the radio playing downstairs in the kitchen. It was soft slow sad music and my insides caved in, and I wanted to die for New Jersey. I got dressed and ate and went outside to see what was happening.

The Johnson's gray maid called to me from a first floor window.

"Hi Nosie," she said. "How are you doing today?"

I walked over and stood under the window looking up at her. We had never talked.

"Hi," I said.

"What trouble are you going to get in today?" she said, laughing.

"I don't know. There's nothing to do around here."

"Don't I know it! But you'll find something. Who all lives over there? Just you, your mother and father?"

"I have a brother but he's in college, and now he's at a summer job. He's a camp counselor in Massachusetts."

"What's his name?"

"Jason. I'm Mildred."

Her head flew back and she started laughing again, real hard, her white teeth flashing.

I smiled. "What's so funny?"

"Oh Nosie," she said, "I am Mildred *too!*"

Then we both laughed.

"Of course I'm really called Milly. You can call me Milly."

"O.K.," I said. I coughed. "I'm called Mildew."

"Mildew?"

"All my friends in New Jersey called me Mildew. Allison and Jerry and Lynne. They were my friends."

She shook her head. She wasn't laughing anymore.

"Well," she said, "isn't that nice. I think that's real nice. You miss them a lot, don't you? And they called you Mildew. That is real nice. Maybe you should keep that as a memory of your friends? Maybe I should just keep calling you Nosie?"

"Well O.K.," I said. "I like Nosie too."

"'Course I know and you know it's not as nice as Mildew. Hey, don't you want to ask me what I do on my day off?"

"Why, what do you do?"

"I'm just teasing you 'cause you haven't asked. It's the first question usually. I don't know what's so fascinating about a maid's day off but everyone wants to know what we do on it."

"Well, what do you do?" I insisted.

Milly laughed again. "Nothing!" she said. "You run along and get in trouble. I've got things to do. Stop by when you see me shaking rugs or sweeping the walk. We can talk." She waved.

"O.K. I will, Milly," I said.

I went to the third floor in the afternoon, adjusted the telescope and scanned the neighborhood. Old Man Porter was messing around in the Bathrobe's garbage can. It looked like he was counting something. I must remember to find out what.

Then I moved to the other window and watched my mother planting the flats of midget marigolds that we had bought at the United Market. The man in the nursery section suggested we buy snail pellets but Mother said, "No, I couldn't kill anything. I can't even swat a fly." Actually she was afraid a dog or cat or little children would eat the pellets. My mother worries about things other people wouldn't even think of. I watched her separate the yellow and orange flowers and plant them all along the back fence. They looked so pretty all in a row. I counted about sixty-four. Mother stood up and wiped her forehead. She smiled, satisfied, then got the garden hose and watered them.

I moved the telescope back to the front window. I got the tripod adjusted just in time to see a green and white taxi pull up by the Calloway's front porch.

A tall and slightly rounded old lady wearing a pink-flowered hat paid the driver and walked through the roses to the front door. She rang the bell. The taxi varoomed and flew up the street.

The lady yanked down her girdle and smoothed her blue dress. The door opened. I couldn't see if it was Mr. or Mrs. Calloway who opened it. But I could see the old lady start to talk, real fast. She must have stood there talking for three minutes straight. Then I saw a hand come out, obviously Irene's, to shake the old lady's hand. Then she went inside.

She was a stranger, I thought, otherwise Irene would have let her in right away or dashed out and hugged her or something. So I reminded myself to ask later who the visitor was.

Now I know you don't think that is much, dear diary. But here is what happened an hour later.

The pink-flowered hat lady came out on the porch, and Dan and Irene came out and stood with her a few minutes until another green and white taxi pulled up to the curb. They all shook hands again, and the lady got in the cab. They waved goodbye, and the taxi took off.

I thought that was the end of it till about ten minutes later when I spied a pink-flowered hat bobbing around in the Calloway's backyard. It moved slowly and slyly from rosebush to rosebush, bobbing around then disappearing completely. I could see Irene and Dan in the front of the house, clipping and petting and talking to the roses there.

I zoomed the telescope back to the backyard roses. There she was. The lady dressed in blue. She made her way to the garage, walked up the outside stairs and *went in* the garage apartment.

My heart jumped — plop — into my mouth. The first thing I wanted to do was call the police. But I got in trouble doing that sort of thing in New Jersey. I called the fire department when our next door neighbor's house was on fire. They came out and chopped down her side door to find her inside and the smoke being steam from her clothes dryer vent. It takes seventy-nine weeks of allowance to pay for a chopped side door.

But someone had sneaked into the Calloway's garage apartment, and I had a pretty good idea she was a lady burglar. So I waited, watching, for an hour so I wouldn't miss seeing her steal silverware or clocks or whatever things the Calloways might have in their garage apartment. But she didn't come out. I saw Irene and Dan in their dining room having dinner. Then Mother called me for dinner. I didn't want to leave the telescope but she said I'd either eat dinner or go straight to bed.

As it turned out, I ate dinner and then had to go straight to bed. I held my eyes open for what seemed like years till Mother and Dad went to bed; then I sneaked back to the third floor for another look.

The Calloway house was dark. But there was a faint flicker of light shining out of the dormer window in the garage apartment! It was scary. So she is still hiding there!

I crept back down the stairs and into bed. And now if I shake when I write this, it's because I am thinking the lady in the pink-flowered hat may be an axe murderer, and if she is, I will be responsible for the blood shed in the Calloway house this night.

Dear Diary, why would an old lady be hiding in the Calloway's garage apartment?

Mildred

❀ I woke up this morning to the sounds of scream-ing. They were coming from our backyard. I ran to look. It was my mother acting like a Russian dancer, stomping and shouting along the back fence. The marigolds were gone. Completely gone. Even the leaves were gone. Only small limp stalks remained. And there were plumpy snails at the bottom of each stalk, sleeping off the feast.

"You ravenous monsters!" my mother screeched, stomping on them. "You gluttonous pigs!" and what I loved best was "You garbage trucks!"

I could hear their shells snap, crackle and pop as her foot came down on them, and I didn't think I wanted to eat breakfast. My mother has a lot more killer in-stinct in her than she realizes. I ran down to the back door as she came in the house. She was slightly out of breath, and her face was all red.

"Mother, when are Pa-Pa and Nana coming to visit?"

She looked at me sort of startled. "Why do you ask, honey?"

"Because I was thinking about them. And I miss them, and I think you need your mother."

"Oh that," she said, nodding to the backyard. She

shrugged her shoulders. "The marigolds looked so beautiful yesterday. Didn't they look beautiful?"

I nodded.

"But, honey, I don't need my mother when I have you. You are more grown up than I, aren't you Mildred?" she teased.

I smiled back. I have a lovely mom. "Sometimes I'm more grown up and sometimes you're more grown up, and we're going to buy snail pellets next time."

She laughed. "Right!" she said.

Sometimes it does seem like I'm the mother and she's my daughter. Sometimes my mother seems sort of helpless. Like in New Jersey on cold days. She couldn't decide what I should wear to school. Most mothers say "You will wear that and that and that." But my mother was never sure. She would always ask me what I thought was best. "Do you think it's cold enough to wear a sweater under your snow suit?" or "Should you wear your boots today or are your shoes enough?" I make all those decisions. Once when Jason broke his arm in school it was up to me to decide which hospital we should go to. I guess some people just can't make decisions. Jason is sort of like mother, maybe that's why she didn't ask him.

I miss Jason. It would help if he were here. He is the kind of brother that takes you with him where he goes and doesn't mind a bit. But I didn't want to think about missing Jason so I ran up to the third floor while Mom fixed breakfast.

I focused the telescope in on the Calloway house. I saw Irene and Dan come out of the house and go to work.

I ran down to eat my breakfast then ran back up again to see if I could see the lady in the garage apartment. I watched the dormer window all morning till I thought my eyes would pop out of my head. I could even see the bees on the roses. But I didn't see the lady till about noon.

She was near the window at the top of the garage having a cup of tea. Dad's telescope is very good. It was Constant Comment tea. I felt brave and decided to question the suspect. So I went downstairs and across the street. I went behind the bay tree, up the outdoor stairway (one step was broken) and knocked on the Calloway's garage apartment door.

She didn't answer. So I peeked in the window. I spied her squatting behind a green summer chair. I felt even braver. I rapped at the window. "Open up. I see you."

She stood up and moved out from behind the green wicker chair. She motioned me away.

"Go away; go away, little girl," she said.

"Let me in," I said. "I want to talk with you."

"Please just go away," she said.

"I have to talk with you."

She shook her head no.

"Do you want me to call the police?" I said.

She came to the door. "I didn't think children could be so . . . ."

"I'm Mildred Murphy. May I come in?"

She stood aside. "Delighted to have you, I'm sure," she said. But I could tell she didn't mean it.

Inside I surveyed the Calloway's garage apartment. It looked more or less like a junk shop, full of things nobody in her right mind would want, all piled in a heap except for the falling apart green wicker chair and chaise lounge that seemed to have been pulled out of the heap.

"This is a nice apartment," I said.

She nodded. "What do you want?"

"What's your name?" I asked.

"Gertie Wilson. Now please, what is it you want? I value my privacy. I was just ready to take a nap when you knocked."

"Is that why you didn't want to answer?"

"Yes, I'm very tired," she said.

I could tell she was lying. "I *love* Constant Comment tea," I said.

She touched her hands together and looked sharply and suspiciously at me. "Well all right," she said, pretty grudgingly, "let's have a cup then."

There is a miniature kitchen in the apartment. On the miniature stove she brewed the tea; then we sat down, Mrs. W. on the chaise and me on the green wicker chair. We sipped at our tea.

"I'm from New Jersey," I said.

"That's nice," she said. Her fingers tapped the wrinkles in her neck.

"Where are you from?"

Her teacup shook noisily. "Why here. Right here."

"But you weren't always here. You just came yesterday. Who are you?"

"Mrs. Calloway's mother was a childhood friend of mine. I came to California to visit her. I didn't know that she had died."

"Are you going to live here now?" I asked.

"What's that? Oh. Oh yes, yes, I am."

"Why?" I said.

Gertie Wilson stood up. "Now you really must go, dear. I've let you in and you've had your tea. I really must rest now. Please go, child."

She didn't seem like she was going to steal anything. She seemed more like a mixed-up old lady.

"It was a pleasure to meet you. Thank you for the tea," I said politely.

Then I raced back home and up to the telescope where I watched her wash up the teacups and lie down on the chaise.

There is definitely something wrong. Mrs. Wilson isn't telling the truth but I don't think she's really a bad person. What I feel inside is that she's a good person but she's telling lies to protect someone, possibly herself. After all, *police* was like a magic word to her. And I did see her *sneak* into the garage apartment.

Dear diary, this is not the end of the Gertie Wilson matter. I shall investigate further tomorrow.

Love, Mildred

P.S. I had to get up for some oatmeal cookies and my old stuffed Bunny toy. They calm me down. I need

that these nights because when I lie down and close my eyes I think of my friends in New Jersey. All I can remember now of Jerry are his beady little eyes. He's only five, but we let him play with us. It doesn't matter how old people are. It only matters if you like them or not. All I can think of about Lynne are her dirty fingernails. But she was nice. Sometimes I see Allison's whole face. It's pretty clear at first then it starts to jump around and jumble. That isn't so bad. What I hate is when it starts to fade. I can't even think what she looks like and she's my best friend. It fades and fades as if there really isn't an Allison at all. I wish Allison would stop fading.

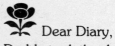 Dear Diary,

Daddy took the day off from work so we could go up to our new house and see how it's coming along. Mom packed a picnic lunch and told me to take some games in case I got bored.

Daddy had a ball poking around the building and explaining to Mom and me which rooms were to be which and then being nervous over when the workers would arrive.

The kitchen-eating area, dining room, living room and Mom and Dad's bedroom all face out to the view and they all open onto the big deck. My room, Jason's room, the bathroom and the kitchen-cooking area face to the street.

It was fun poking around for awhile. Mother took a camp chair out to the deck and enjoyed the view. Daddy pestered the workers as to when the house would be done and could he drive a few nails, etc. I expect he drove them crazy, and I know they hope he never takes another day off.

I went out on the deck to ask Mom if I could look around the neighborhood.

"Sure, honey. Have a nice walk. You won't get lost?"

"Daddy is really nuts over this house, isn't he?"

"You noticed. Yes, he's quite proud of it, and it *will* be lovely," my mother said.

"But it really doesn't mean that much to you, does it?"

She glanced at me then back out to the view of the hills and the San Pablo Bay. "Well, it does mean a lot to me because Daddy loves it. But I could live anywhere; I guess you know that. I could live in a shack. But that's our secret."

"Don't you want to come with me and meet some of our neighbors?" I don't know why I asked. I knew she wouldn't. She's kind of a loner.

She smiled. "Go *on* now! Wander back when you get hungry. I'm busy falling in love with this view."

So I went up on the road, and the first person I saw was this funny-looking kid called Nancy. She had the biggest freckles I ever saw, as big as the red polka dots on her shorts. And she had hardly any hair and what there was of it was red, except it was really orange.

"What's the matter with you?" I said.

"I'm just getting over ringworm," she said. "Do you want to play?"

"Sure," I said.

Nancy is nine, and she'll be in fourth grade, and we have decided to be best friends when I move in, which according to Daddy will be about four months and according to the builder, ten months. We played all morning, and I took her back to the new house to share our picnic lunch. My mother got a funny look on her face when she saw Nancy's head and the messy medicine on it.

Then we went back to Nancy's, and I fell in a patch of poison oak, and her mother made me take a shower, and I had to sit around in Nancy's father's bathrobe while her mother washed and dried my clothes. I found out that the rest of the kids from the hill were in summer school.

"Is everybody dumb up here?" I asked.

Nancy didn't know what I meant. It seems everybody in California *loves* summer school, and they are all dying to go, and Nancy is just sick that she couldn't. And guess what I found out? Mrs. Murchison is Nancy's mother's aunt! Small world. I suppose I will have to love to go to summer school next year, too. Isn't that depressing?

"How come everyone wants to go to summer school?" I asked.

Nancy shrugged her shoulders. "We just do."

"But when the weather is so nice in the summer, that's the time to *play*. In New Jersey all we wanted to do was play all summer and go on vacation and things like that. We hated summer school."

"The weather's always nice here," Nancy said.

I hadn't thought of that. Maybe that's the answer. Or maybe their teachers brainwashed them from kindergarten on, and they just don't know any better.

When I got back to the new house Mom and Dad were in the car ready to go and wondering where I was. All Daddy said was, "Ringworm *and* poison oak?

Good God." But I found out he was in a foul mood because one of the carpenters had threatened to quit if he didn't go away and stop pestering.

When we got back to our old rented house, the Calloways were home from work and busy with their roses. I wandered over to ask a few questions about Gertie You-Know-Who.

"Yellow roses are my favorite," I said.

Irene looked up, surprised, and I think, pleased. "Are they, Mildred? They were the favorite of my mother too."

Then Dan and his chin gave me a five minute talk on the history and breeding of the yellow rose.

"You should teach summer school," I said. "All the kids go around here. You could teach *Roses.*"

Neither of them seemed to think it was a good idea.

"I saw the taxi cab at your house Sunday," I said. "Was it a friend of your mother's visiting?"

"Why yes it was," Irene said. "How perceptive. It was a Mrs. Wilson from Detroit, Michigan. She was an old friend of Mother's and I had heard Mother speak of her but I had never met her."

"Where is she now?" I asked.

Irene's face turned chalk white. "Why buried. You know, she died."

"Mrs. Wilson!"

"Oh. I thought you meant Mother. I'm sorry, Mildred. No, Mrs. Wilson is fine I suppose. She said she was on her way to see Disneyland."

I swallowed and probably turned chalk white too.

"You didn't ask her to stay and visit?" I asked. They both looked at me like I was out of my mind. "Well, so long," I sort of mumbled. I ran across the street and up to the third floor and barrelled the telescope in on the little garage apartment. I set it to extra powerful. The sun was wrong for me but definitely, yes, a shadow the size of Gertie Wilson was moving around up there! I watched so long I fell asleep and only woke up when Mom called me for dinner.

Dear Diary, what do you think? What do you think?

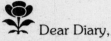 Dear Diary,

I was just sitting on the front steps this morning trying to get up courage to go over and confront Gertie Wilson when Milly, the Johnson's maid, appeared before me all dressed up in a rose-colored suit.

"Hi Nosie," she said. "Do you recognize me? It's my day off!" Then she laughed.

"Hi," I said. "You look pretty!"

"Listen, little one, I know you're having a real boring time in this old falling-down neighborhood. Ask your Momma can you come to San Francisco with next-door Milly."

I jumped up. "Honest?" I said. Then I ran screaming for Mom.

She said I could go but she made me change into my blue dress and take a coat because it's cold in San Francisco even in the summer, and I had to take a pocketbook with money to pay my own way. And I had to wear knee socks.

Milly and I walked down to the bus station where we got a bus that wound around through lots of hills and towns in Marin County then crossed the Golden Gate Bridge and ended up in San Francisco.

The first thing we did was take a cable car and get off

in Chinatown. We went in and out of about fifty shops, and I bought Daddy some incense and a burner, and Mom a teapot and cups, and Jason a carved ivory monkey. Then we took another cable car down to Fisherman's Wharf. Milly had a shrimp cocktail as we walked along the sidewalk (I ate her crackers), then we went in a restaurant, and she had abalone. I had spaghetti and a loaf and a half of sour dough bread.

"I like your day off," I said.

"You're supposed to eat fish at Fisherman's Wharf," she said.

"The only fish I like is tuna fish sandwiches," I said. "Is this what you do every day off? Don't you visit your family?"

"I guess maybe I don't have any family anymore," Milly said. "Leastways I don't know."

"You don't know? Weren't you ever married?"

"Oh yes." Milly laughed. "I was that. Married. Once."

"Did you have children?"

"I suppose. But now, where are they gone? I don't know. My daughter be about forty-five now. Two boys even older. They're gone into the air. Vanished. I don't know about them. I've got the Johnson's. They're my family now. The only one I got."

"It must be awful not to know. It sounds so lonely."

"I think you'll find everybody's lonely in their own way. Do you want me to ask for more bread?"

I shook my head no.

"Well, let's get on then. I want to show you the

aquarium in Golden Gate Park then we'll have a cup of strong tea at the Japanese Gardens and head for home. That sound o.k. to you?"

"It sounds great!" I said.

And it was. On the way home in the bus I remembered to ask Milly what Old Man Porter could have been doing in Bathrobe's garbage can.

"Counting bottles, is likely," she said.

"What do you mean?" I said.

"Mrs. Houghton is an alcoholic. She drinks. All day long maybe all night long for all I know."

"She watches TV too," I said.

Milly laughed. "So you've been spying on her? Poor soul!"

"I didn't even know it was a *her*. Why does she drink anyway?"

Milly shook her head. "Who knows?"

I had to tell Mom all about San Francisco, and when I was done I still had time to talk to Gertie before the Calloways would come home from work.

The garage apartment door opened before I could even knock on it.

"Say," Gertie whispered and whisked me inside, "what were you talking to the Calloways about yesterday?"

So, she was worried.

"We discussed yellow roses," I said.

"And me?"

"Well, sort of," I said.

"Did you tell them?"

"What?"

She sat down on the wicker chaise and shook her head. "Oh dear, how much do you know? Don't play games with an old lady."

She looked perky but her knees wobbled as she sat there. I told her all I saw and that the Calloways think she is in Disneyland. She looked like she was thinking real hard.

"Gosh, what's wrong? Tell me what's wrong and what you're doing and I'll help you. I like you. I don't care what you are, a burglar or anything. I'll help you."

She looked at me hard, and then she started to laugh. "I'm not a burglar, honey. I'm just flat broke."

And then she told me all about it, how she only gets sixty-eight dollars a month from social security and that she had savings of ten thousand dollars when her husband died but how that dwindled down to four hundred dollars and she was about to be evicted if she couldn't pay her rent so she spent about two hundred dollars to come to California because her friend (Irene's mother) had told her to come out and live in the apartment over the garage. Then she got here and the mother was dead and hadn't mentioned her living there to Irene and Dan. In fact when Gertie asked them about the garage apartment, Dan and Irene had looked terribly embarrassed. They implied that something was really wrong with the garage. But they wouldn't say what it was. Anyhow, Gertie was desperate for a place to sleep so she got out of the cab two blocks away, sneaked back to the garage and is secretly living there.

"What do you think is wrong with the garage apartment?"

"Nothing as far as I can see. Just dirty and old and kind of rickety," Gertie said. "There were a mess of California ants, but I got rid of them. Even the little appliances work. I can't imagine why but they certainly made a fuss about how no one could live in the apartment. I think they probably just didn't want me around."

"Do you sleep on that bed over there?" I asked. "It has so much junk piled on it."

"Oh no," Gertie said, "that's where the ants were. Besides the floor squeaks over there and sort of sags under the bed. See? I sleep on the chaise."

"It looks uncomfortable. What do you eat?" I asked.

"I had a bag of apples in my suitcase. I love apples. But they're almost gone. I found a few condiments in the cupboards here. Spices, the tea. Nothing to eat, really. I want to go to the store. Of course I don't know where the store is."

"I'll go," I said.

"Then I've got to get to the Post Office so my social security check will come here."

"I'll go to the Post Office," I said.

"And I'd like to pay for the water I use and the electricity, you know. It was all shut off. I turned it on. I want to pay. But how can I do that without them knowing?"

"Could you casually leave it in their mailbox?" I said, but I knew it was a dumb answer.

"You know, I think it will work if you help me," she said.

"I'll try," I promised. "But how long can you keep living here without telling them? And what will you do on Saturdays and Sundays when they're home? When they might come out to the garage for tools or something?"

"I'm very resourceful. I'll think of something," she promised.

"What does that door go to?" I asked.

"It's a stairway down to the garage. Rickety." She jumped up and looked at her watch. "Hurry you must go. They'll be home from work soon. I wouldn't want them to catch you around here!"

"Do you want me to go to the grocery store and Post Office tomorrow?" I asked.

"Yes, dear, thank you. I'm so lucky to have you helping me. It's going to be fun."

I left and felt mysterious all the way across the street, like a spy. I have a big secret inside me. I, Mildred Murphy, who has never been able to keep a secret in my life. I am being trusted. It's weird.

Love, Mildred

I got a letter from Allison today. Allison used to talk so much I sometimes felt like shouting SHUT UP, ALLISON! This is what she said in her letter.

Dear Mildew,
How are you? I am fine. I miss you. How is California? How is your mother? How is your dad? How is your brother? I have to put my dog out.
Love, Allison

I can't believe it; she says the same thing in all her letters. I never did like her dog. When I was six he ate my green tennis shoes.

Gertie keeps Everett's picture (he was her husband) under her pillow, and every night she pulls it out and cries for him. She says it is the only thing that gets her down. It must be terrible to be old and lose someone you love. She says she'll never get over Everett being gone, and I believe it. She talks about him all the time.

Gertie also showed me some pictures of herself. Some were when she was very young.

"People used to say I looked like a movie star," she said. "Do you see it? Who do you suppose it was?"

"Well," I said. I had no idea.

"Maybe you didn't know her. Marjorie Main. They

said we looked quite a bit alike when I was young and she was young. Now do you know who I'm always mistaken for?"

"Who?"

"Someone on TV. She cooks things on TV. She has cookbooks you can buy in a store. Everytime I go into a bookstore, they want me to autograph a few cookbooks. Do you watch The French Chef, Julia Child?"

"No, but my grandmother does and she says she licks the spoons and puts them back in the drawer," I said.

"I'm often mistaken for Julia Child," Gertie said.

"Oh," I said.

I went to the grocery store today and bought her three eggs, ¼ lb. butter, a jar of dried beef, Constant Comment Tea, a bag of apples, peanut butter and crackers.

At the Post Office I filled out a card for her social security check to be mailed in care of General Delivery. I also went to the drug store for some headache pills.

"You don't know how I'd love to make a pie or some homemade bread to surprise the Calloways with when they come home from work," Gertie said when I arrived with the bundles. "I make the best cookies, too, and jams and jellies. I used to make cookies all the time in Michigan and give them to the police and firemen. I lived near City Hall. How they loved my cookies."

Gertie brewed two cups of tea. After we drank it she washed and dried the cups and put them on the shelf.

"Do you play cards?" she asked.

She found a deck in her suitcase, and we played all my favorite games and then she taught me how to play Solitaire about three different ways.

"Maybe you could bake a pie someday just for you and me to eat," I suggested.

Gertie thought it was a great idea.

"Lemon? Pumpkin? Apple? Cherry? What's your favorite?" she said.

"Blueberry."

"Then blueberry it is. You can go to the store tomorrow and get the ingredients then come here and we'll bake and eat a blueberry pie! Big or small?" she said.

"Oh, *big*," I said.

"Did I tell you I have a daughter?" Gertie said.

"No!"

"Yes. Janet. A lovely girl."

"Where is she? Why don't you live with her?"

"Oh I couldn't do that. No. No. She has a family. A nice family in Detroit. Her husband's name is Guy. Well, I might as well be honest with you, Mildred. The fact is they haven't asked me to live with them. Of course I wouldn't. You can love someone and still not want to live with them. I understand that. And I keep my financial problems to myself."

"Do you have . . ."

"Grandchildren?" she finished. "Oh do I? The most adorable darlings you ever did see."

And then she showed me their pictures. There were four of them. Timothy in his football uniform, 7. Greta in the swimming pool, 5. Lisa doing a somersault, 3.

And Sean who was just sitting and quite fat, 1½.

"What will they do without you?" I said.

"Why they'll do just fine. They aren't ninnies. And when I figure out a way to make some money, I'll go for a trip to visit them."

Tonight at dinner I asked Mom and Dad, "What kind of a job could a sixty-seven-year old lady get?"

My dad said, "Eat your peas."

"I'm *eating* them," I said.

"That's an interesting question," my mother said. "Is it anyone we know? Sixty-seven is a little old to go job hunting."

"It's a hypotenuse question," I said.

"Hypothetical," Dad said. "Is the supposed person in good health?"

"Yes, but perhaps we could say she has arthritus in the morning. I don't think she could work real hard. But suppose she is flat broke and needs cash right now."

"Well," Dad said, "I would think she would be getting social security, medicare, probably a pension if her husband worked. I assume she's widowed."

"I think we could say he died before getting a pension. And maybe she only gets sixty-eight dollars in social security and has used up her savings?" I said.

"It certainly sounds like a definite person to me," Mother said.

"Forget it," I said. "I was just making up problems and trying to solve them."

"I don't see the hypothetical person getting a job, do you dear?" Mom asked Dad.

"Perhaps babysitting now and then," Dad said.

He stood up from the table. It was my night to do dishes. Babysitting, I thought. Well it would be something. But how could people get in touch with Gertie? They'd have to know where she lived. She'd have to sneak in and out of the garage apartment. She doesn't even have a phone. No, that wouldn't do. I'd have to get her a daytime job. I thought about going down to the bakery and seeing if they would hire her. Maybe we could lie about her age? No, she *looks* sixty-seven. Maybe we could dye her hair and powder over her wrinkles?

The dishes done, I kissed Mom and Dad goodnight and came upstairs to take my bath. I did an old trick where you run the water. Wait five minutes. Then drain the tub. Fools them all the time!

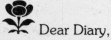 Dear Diary,

Gertie was laughing when I went over this morning.

"Hiding out in someone's garage apartment is surely one of the worst fixes I've managed to get into, in a long, long time," she said. She looked at the ceiling of the apartment. There is a lot of black dust clinging to the ceiling. "I need some fresh air even if it is risky going outdoors. Let's take a walk before any of that black sooty stuff falls on our heads."

"O.K. Come to the store with me. Get some fresh air. Now don't worry, *nobody will see you*. That big bay tree hides the outside stairs almost completely."

So we both sneaked out of the garage apartment, courtesy of the bay tree. I went first and Gertie came five minutes later. We met two blocks away and walked downtown.

"Oh it's a nice town," she said. "Oh look over there! It's a pretty town."

At the market we bought blueberries, tapioca, sugar, flour and butter. We might have bought some other things, too, but I can't remember. Gertie had forgotten her list, but she said she was sure there was some nutmeg and cinnamon at the garage.

On the way home we walked by a church, a shoe

shop and a furniture store. When we got near the bookstore Gertie looked all bubbly and said, "Why don't we go inside?"

We got in the door, and she poked me with her elbow and whispered, "Wait till they get a look at me."

We walked around the store pretending to look at books. I looked at the clerk, and he looked at us but nothing happened. It didn't bother Gertie. She just walked around with a mysterious smile on her face. Then finally she walked to the cookbooks, picked up three by Julia Child and walked to the counter.

"I'm just passing through," she said with the sweetest smile. "Love your store; suppose you won't mind if I autograph a few books for you?"

The clerk stared at her. Gertie pointed to the picture of Julia Child then she pointed to her own face. Then she autographed three books!

The clerk looked befuddled then grateful. "Thank you, Ms. Child," he said.

"No trouble," Gertie said, graciously. "Glad to do it."

Before I knew it we were out on the street walking along and Gertie was so happy and talking, talking, talking. I couldn't believe it. Of course she never actually *said* she was Julia Child but she certainly led the clerk to believe it.

She wasn't too happy when we got back to the garage and discovered she had forgotten to get a lemon. I said that was no problem. I could get one from Old Man Porter because he is always outside his little yellow house handing them out anyhow. Back down the stairs. I slithered through the shadow of the bay tree and when it looked safe I walked over to his place.

He was picking withered brown blossoms off his geraniums and glad to give me a lemon. He thought it was for my mother, so I went straight home and around to the backyard. I put the lemon in my halter, did a zig-zag walk, very casually, even going two blocks out of my way, then back to the garage. If Old Man Porter didn't notice I had one bosom in the middle of my halter, he wouldn't suspect a thing.

Gertie was so happy making the pie, she sang.

"Now I'm doing what I love," she said. She also licks her spoons.

"It smells good," I said.

And it was. We both ate two pieces. I didn't realize the time. It was late. When I went out the door a chunk of molding broke off in my hand.

"I'm sorry," I said to Gertie. "I'll bring a hammer and nails tomorrow to fix it."

As I left the garage Dan Calloway came home from work and saw me coming out from behind the bay tree! I know I looked guilty and panicky and horrible.

He had this huge smile on his face and he looked so happy to see me. "Mildred, Mildred, how nice to see you. Are you having fun? Do you like California? Let me share my good news with you."

I waited.

"We just found out today. After over a year of hoping and praying we're going to get a baby. A real baby! We're adopting one ready-made. One with booties and bonnets and a little tiny nose." He sighed. "I'm going to be a father. Here, take this cigar and give it to your father. Mildred, will you come and play with our baby?"

"Sure!" I said. "When do you get it?"

He frowned. "That will take a few more months. But we've been accepted by the adoption agency. The next baby born, boy or girl, twins or triplets, will belong to us!"

"That's really nice," I said.

Then he leaned over and put his arm on my shoulder. "Mildred, just one thing, don't play around the garage anymore. It's not safe. We're having it torn down."

I caught my breath. "Why are you doing that? It's a nice garage. A beautiful garage. You don't want to tear it down!"

Dan shook his head sadly. "Termites," he whispered.

"Termites?" I said. I remembered the chunk of wood that had broken off in my hand, the black dust on the ceiling. My grandparent's front porch had termites once.

"It's very dangerous. We had a young couple renting there about a year ago and they discovered the termites. They moved out that very day. Discovered we had some in the house too but the exterminators got those. The garage was too far gone. We thought it would fall down before we got it torn down. But we wanted to wait till Irene's mother passed on. Couldn't tell her. It was sentimental to her. She lived there, she and her husband as bride and groom while the big house was being built. Guess you didn't know that it's fixed up like a little apartment upstairs. It was her honeymoon cottage sort of thing. We couldn't tell her it was being eaten by termites."

I tried not to look like my whole world had caved in. But I couldn't stop the shaking of my body. "When . . . are . . . you . . . tearing it down?" I asked, weakly.

"In a week or two," Dan said. "I have a friend with a bulldozer and he's not sure when he can come."

"Is it really dangerous?" I asked.

He nodded yes.

"I have to go home," I said.

"Don't forget about our baby!" Dan said, smiling.

I waved the cigar at him. "Congratulations," I said.

Dan watched me all the way across the street so I had no chance to tell Gertie that her California ants were termites! And that the garage is in falling-down condition.

Then after dinner I thought I could sneak over and tell her but Mother wanted to go to the movies. It's very late.

I hope Gertie will be safe tonight. If she isn't, I'll die. I have to wake up early tomorrow morning so I can tell Gertie about the garage and she can get out before it's torn down.

Where will she go? With no money?

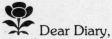 Dear Diary,
I woke up this morning with my mother's hand patting my shoulder.

"Mildred, honey. Mildred," she whispered.

I opened my eyes.

"Daddy wants us to go into San Francisco with him to pick out the light fixtures for the new house."

"Light fixtures?" I said.

"And cabinet pulls, door knobs, things like that. Linoleum."

"Linoleum?" I said. I don't wake up very fast.

"For the new house. Come on, honey," my mother said. "If you don't jump out of bed this minute I'm going to hire a bulldozer to drag you out." She smiled.

I smiled. "Bulldozer?" I said. Then, I *jumped* out of bed. "Bulldozer!" I said.

"Mildred, you're babbling. What are you talking about? Are you sleep walking or are you awake?"

"I think I'm half-awake," I said. "The half that's awake knows I can't go with you today. The other half isn't sure why," I said. Or isn't telling, I thought.

My mother frowned. "You mean you think there is something you have to do today but you can't re-member what it is?"

I nodded.

"You should write yourself notes, Mildred. That's what I do."

"Do I have to go?" I asked.

"Well, you don't *have* to. We thought you might like to . . . help decide," Mother said.

"I don't want to go." I said.

"Well."

"I'm old enough. You let Jason stay by himself when he was ten."

"Well," my mother said.

My father said I could stay. He said he would bring mother home after their lunch in Chinatown. I guess they thought when I heard that I would change my mind. I would like to have lunch in Chinatown. But not TODAY.

As soon as my mother and father left, I ran over to tell Gertie Wilson the horrible news about the termites eating at the garage and the bulldozer that would come in a week or so to tear it all down.

Gertie pretended that the news didn't bother her but I know it did because her knees began to shake and wobble.

"So that's why this old garage seems to be falling apart," I said. "It *is* falling apart. Gertie, you're not safe and the bulldozer is coming. What are we going to do?"

"I'll have to gather up my things and leave," Gertie whispered.

"Maybe you could live in my house, on the third

floor. My parents hardly go up there. They're not home this morning."

"Oh no. I don't want to complicate your life. I don't want you to have to lie to your family. You have such a nice little family. No, I'll just leave and go . . . somewhere," Gertie said.

She sat and just thought for a few minutes. Then she sighed. "The only thing left for me to do is take the money I have left, go on the bus as near as it will take me to Detroit, then phone Janet to come and get me. I'll tell her I'm broke. I'll be dependent on her when I want so much to be independent. I'll be *poor old Grandmother Wilson hasn't got two dimes to rub together.* Well, we all find ourselves in some situation when we're old. This is mine."

"Gertie, I wish you wouldn't give up. We have some time," I said. "We can think of a plan."

"I'm old enough to know there's no magic answer, Mildred." Then she told me I better go home. "My quarters are a dangerous place. If this all collapses around me, it won't matter. But you, Mildred, mustn't be hurt."

I told her I'd try to think of something. She smiled bravely.

What do you think, Diary? Is there any magic left for lonely old people?

I need some lunch.

Love, Mildred

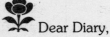 Dear Diary,

My mother and dad got a lot done in San Francisco and they had a nice lunch in Chinatown. They each ordered and ate their own lunch because my mother gets nervous if she orders something she likes and then someone starts spooning it on their plate and eating it. My father understands.

And surprise! This afternoon, Nancy came to visit her great-aunt, Mrs. Murchison, so she came over to play with me.

Her hair is beginning to grow back in, there isn't so much medicine showing, and she looks more like a human being than the first time I met her.

"Can you keep a secret?" I asked.

Nancy nodded her head and her eyes doubled in size. She really looked like the kind of kid who would blab almost anything, but I had to tell someone, so I told her.

We sat down on the grass under the palm tree and I told her all about Gertie Wilson and how she was living in the condemned garage.

"Oh my gosh," Nancy kept saying. Then she said, "What are you going to do?"

"I don't know," I said.

"Well I won't tell anyone," Nancy said. "I promise."

"If we could just think of a way to help Gertie," I said.

"You mean make her rich so she'd never have any more troubles?" Nancy asked.

"She only needs a place to live and a little money. That's all she needs. It's so simple. But we can't find the answer and there she sits in that termity garage."

"My great-aunt would know what to do. She says there's no problem that can't be solved with smiles all around," Nancy said.

"Mrs. Murchison does have a nice smile," I said.

"My father says she's a busybody," Nancy said. "But my mother says she really cares about people. I bet she would know how to help your Mrs. Wilson."

"Well, I'll think about it," I said. "I don't exactly want to tell the whole world about Gertie."

"You need something to take your mind off your problems. Do you have any games? What do you want to do?"

I thought. "We could play gift shop," I said.

"I don't know that game," Nancy said.

"It's easy. We go in our living room and that's our gift shop. We own it. We're business partners. We sell the furniture and ashtrays and lamps and curtains to pretend people who come in our shop."

I grabbed a brick from the patio. "This can be our cash register and we'll also write down prices of everything so we'll know how much they cost when people ask."

"I never played it," Nancy said.

"Maybe it's a New Jersey game. C'mon. It's fun," I said.

Nancy liked the game and she really made me laugh because she can fake the voice of a rich lady and it's so funny to look at Nancy and hear this voice coming out of her.

"My deah, you really must rush these items to me. I need them passionately. Ten millionaires are coming to dinner tonight and I want everything to look simply splendid."

She'll probably be an actress when she grows up like a lady my father went to high school with who acts in mouthwash commercials on TV.

I guess I'm lucky Nancy will be my best friend. I hope it doesn't take too long for our house to be finished. My mother says it's better to have no friends at all if they are people who hurt you or change you or make you miserable. I know there are people like that. And nobody's perfect. But Nancy is nearly perfect and her accent makes me laugh and after we played gift shop we played Milles Bourne and I won. I could never win Milles Bourne in New Jersey. I'm looking forward to our being best friends.

After Nancy left I sneaked over under the bay tree and had another chat with Gertie. The Calloways were in their front yard, so they couldn't see us.

Gertie said the garage roof creaked so bad this afternoon she thought it would fall on top of her! I'm afraid something awful will happen.

"Maybe you should call Janet," I said.

"I'll see how bad it is tonight," she said.

She has no more ideas than I on where she can go. I think she can check into a motel. I don't think they want you to pay until you leave. But Gertie says she can't charge money she doesn't have. She has to save the little cash she has for food. Maybe tonight I'll think of something.

I went up to the third floor after dinner and looked out at the night through the telescope. I saw stars that must be as far away as New Jersey. I thought about space. About planets. I thought about if there were no planets at all, no moons, no stars, nothing nothing anywhere but vast vast space.

Mildred

After breakfast this morning I wandered around the house.

"What are you looking for in the corners of this house?" Mother asked. "Everywhere I go you're staring into corners."

"I don't know," I said.

I went up to the third floor. I looked through the telescope at the Calloway garage. It was looking sturdy enough. I looked very carefully. I couldn't see a termite.

I moved the telescope to the back window. Mrs. Murchison's pink one-piece underwear was still hanging on the clothesline from yesterday. It's made by Munsingwear. Size XL. Milly was sitting at the picnic table in the Johnson's patio. She was looking at the newspaper and writing something on a piece of paper. Correction. She was printing something. CHEER FOR YOUR WASH.

"Hooray," I said.

It didn't seem as funny when the word came out as I thought it was going to be, in my head. Still I couldn't stop.

"Yea, yea wash! Fight on, soapsuds! You've got the spirit, scummy water!"

My eyes felt like crying. I couldn't understand why when my mouth was being so funny. I lay down on the old oriental rug and looked up at the ceiling. There are all kinds of cracks up there. Some of them formed a pretty decent star, and some others looked like half a merry-go-round. I decided to go down to the Johnson's patio to visit with Milly.

The Johnson's have a lot of oleander in their backyard. It is a bush with pretty pink flowers but you must never never never eat a leaf or probably any part of an oleander bush because it is poison!

I guess Milly didn't see me coming from behind the oleander because when she did see me, she jumped and got all nervous and gathered up the newspaper and pencil and the paper she had printed CHEER FOR YOUR WASH on and held them tight to her chest.

"Hi," I said.

"What do you want?" Milly said. She didn't sound as if she liked me anymore.

"Nothing," I said. "I saw you writing down here, and I thought I'd come over and say hi."

"I wasn't writing," Milly said. Her eyes looked around at all the oleander when she said that. Then her eyes looked at my feet as if they were real disgusted at the sight of my blue tennis shoes. "You been spying on me?" she asked. "You and that telescope going to get into trouble."

I sat down on the other side of the picnic table. "I know. Don't be mad at me, Milly. I have enough trouble."

It seemed like she tightened up the hold on the newspaper and her printing paper.

"I've been lying to my mother because I have a secret. In order to keep it a secret, I have to lie," I said.

Milly closed her eyes. She breathed deeply. She opened her eyes. "I know that story," she said. "I lie sometimes too. I did it just now. I lied to you. Yes, I did. I just lied to my little friend, Nosie."

"Do you have a secret too?" I asked.

Milly nodded. She almost seemed relieved. Her shoulders seemed to fall and her lips began to smile.

"I have a secret too," she said.

Milly is all sort of powdery around the mouth. A piece of hair hangs like a question mark from her left ear. With the oleander bushes behind her and the newspaper clutched to her chest she looks like an oil painting that should be in a museum and famous.

"Are you going to tell me your secret?" I asked.

Milly laughed. "Are you going to tell me yours?" she asked.

"But I can't." I said.

She smiled real nice. I knew she wasn't going to tell me her secret either.

"I wish I knew how to stay out of trouble," I said.

"Not enough to keep you busy here," Milly said.

"How did you stay busy when you were ten? How did you stay out of trouble?"

Milly moved her head back and forth. "Lordy, I was never ten. I was always sixty-five."

"What do you mean?" I asked.

"I didn't have time to spare like you. I was always working, helping. Even younger than you. Seems like always."

"Like what?" I said. "Like what did you do?"

"Well," Milly said. She was thinking. She was thinking, I think, how much she would tell me.

"I was the big sister, the oldest of what finally turned out to be nine kids. I was their big sister. But really I was their momma. Our own momma went to work. I was the momma at home. Long as I can remember. When I was eight I remember doing all the stuff a momma does. We lived in Chicago. On a street where there were lots of people, lots of poorness, lots of brick buildings, lots of darkness and rain. Too much heat in the summer made you want to die; too much cold in the winter made you know it's possible to freeze to death in Chicago. Jeremiah Williams across the street did. They didn't have no heat at all that winter. Too much work for a girl of eight, too little food, too much crying from the little kids, too much slapping and yelling at them."

Milly's second finger moved across her upper lip like it would make a groove there. Her eyes were looking at the burls in the picnic table. They didn't see the burls. I think they saw that street in Chicago.

"I guess the worst thing of all that happened was when I was nine and in charge days and nights while our momma was a live-in maid for rich folks. Lil Darcy, he was one of the boys; oh, he was about four years old. He took to lighting matches. We darned near all burnt up. It's hard to think about. But we all got out O.K. It was one of the firemen who died, saving us. All I could say to Darcy for two weeks was 'Damn you, Darcy. Damn your soul.' "

She sighed. "We moved to another apartment in the building. We didn't have a regular daddy. We had one now and then. Just as well. They liked to beat up on the kids. And other things. Momma bought me a crystal set. It's like a radio, you know. Sometimes when the bigger kids were off to school and I got all the babies to take a nap, I'd have some time to listen. Them my best times. I'd have killed anybody touched that crystal set. They knew it was Milly's. Finally it was gone. We had to sell it. For food, I think. It's likely."

"Didn't you go to school?" I asked.

Milly's eyes blinked and moved from the burls of the picnic table to my face. "Did I say that?" she asked me.

"No," I said.

She said she had to get back in the house. It was time to start the pot roast. As she got up, something fell out of the clutch of newspaper in her arms. I picked it up. It was a letter. I handed it to Milly.

"From my daughter," she said.

"Then you've heard from her!" I said.

Milly pointed to the postmark. "When does that say?" she said.

"February, 1952," I read. "Oh," I added.

Milly started walking toward the Johnson's house. Suddenly she turned and looked at me. "You want to read it?" she asked.

"Me? Oh no!"

"Go on," she said. "Read it aloud. Slow."

I took the old letter out of the envelope. "Dear Ma," I read. "Jordan got peritonitus. They got him in a hospital. I don't know he'll ever get back to work. I think he's to die. The twins got bad colds. We got to move. Can you send fifty dollars? Ma, I wouldn't ask but we need. Scared without Jordan. Desperate, ma. Love, Desileen."

Milly was crying. She took the letter and stared at it. "Fifty dollars," she said, softly. "I can send that."

"But the letter was written in 1952!" I said.

Milly looked up. "I know," she said, bitterly. "In 1952 I didn't have fifty dollars." Then she walked into the house.

I felt sad again and I remembered why. I don't want Gertie to go to Detroit to be *poor old Grandmother Wilson without two dimes to rub together.* I saw the Calloways drive away in their car so I ran over to see Gertie. She was looking for me. She wanted me to go downtown with her. She had *decided.* She said the part of the floor where the bed was, sagged and groaned worse than ever.

"It's time to be sensible," Gertie said. "The summer of the garage is over."

We went to the phone booth in Poehlman's drugstore. She phoned Janet in Detroit and reversed the charges. She explained what had happened with Irene Calloway's mother and how she had no place to go. And then Gertie told me to talk to Janet.

Janet sounded real nice and told me to tell Gertie to fly home (Janet would pay) and that Janet and Guy would think of something for Gertie, probably a retirement home.

Gertie felt pretty good after the phone call. "I don't mind a retirement home," she said. "I mean, I don't like it, not yet, I'm not ready. But I can accept it."

"Yes."

"I'll do my best to be happy. You know I'll try, don't you Mildred? It's better than a termite-filled garage," Gertie said.

"Yes."

"Old falling down garage," Gertie said.

"Yes. It's better than that," I said. I stuck my finger in my left ear. It was buzzing like it used to in New Jersey.

As we walked by the bookstore Gertie noticed a sign in the window that said they had autographed Julia Child cookbooks for sale. That made her smile.

When we got back to the garage, my head ached and I couldn't get my ear to stop buzzing. I hugged Gertie and told her I loved her.

Gertie said, "Let's not say goodbye yet. I hate to say goodbye. You're taking me to the bus station tomorrow aren't you? We'll say goodbye then."

She went inside to pack. We will get up early and I'll take her downtown to get a bus to San Francisco. Then she'll get another bus to the airport. She'll go to the United ticket counter where Janet will have arranged a ticket for her. Then she'll fly away to her retirement home.

I'll miss you Gertie. And your blueberry pie and wobbly knees. And everything.

Damn you termites. Damn your soul.

Love, Mildred

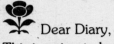 Dear Diary,
This is going to be short because I don't feel so good. I woke up with a terrible headache. I wanted to go see Gertie off at the bus stop but I didn't feel like moving. My ear felt stuffed and it pounded. I told Mother and she took me to a doctor. I got my old New Jersey ear infection back. I have to take red medicine and the doctor's name is Dr. John Happy. And on his nurse's desk a sign says Clare Nuyer. So guess what I thought of? Happy Nu-yer. Get it?

I guess Gertie is on the airplane now on her way to Detroit, Michigan. The whole world feels empty.

My ear hurts. My neck is too sore to turn my head. I'm in bed looking straight ahead. I never think about how nice it is to turn my head until times like this, when I can't. This is when I wonder how many times a day I turn my head when it's turnable. When I get better I'm going to count. Right now I would guess in the thousands.

My grandfather, Pa-Pa, knows a man who can't ever turn his head. If he wants to look around, his whole body goes with his head. My mother told me about it this morning when she came up to see if there was anything I wanted.

His name is Roger Jardine. He used to come and visit Pa-Pa when mother was little. When Roger Jardine was sick from whatever made his neck unable to move, my grandfather gave him blood to save his life. So for all these years Roger Jardine has my grandfather's blood in his body, and he comes to visit my grandfather at least once a year to remind Pa-Pa that he is glad he has his blood and glad he is alive.

My mother says he doesn't say "thank you for saving my life" in words. He just comes to visit. And they talk a bit about old times. And Roger Jardine looks straight ahead or turns his whole body to see something. He sits stiff and walks stiff. I wonder how my grandfather feels to have saved someone's life? I think I would like to do that someday, when I'm feeling better.

My mother also told me about another man who came to visit Pa-Pa and Nana. He had a bushy mustache. His wife was nice, and she knitted. Herbert and Peg Reinburger. But my mother would run and hide when they visited because Herbert was a kissing mess. He loved to kiss ladies and little girls. His kisses were sloppy and mustachy. His mustache would go right up your nose. My mother didn't like Herbert Reinburger but she said she felt sorry for him because he was a phony. He was the first phony she ever met, so I guess she must have met him when she was a baby.

"Don't ever be a phony, Mildred," she said. "Don't ever put-on that you're happy or excited or crazy about someone when you're not. If you're mad, be mad. If you're sad, be sad. If you're glad, be glad."

"I'm sick."

"Good," my mother said. "You do a fine job at it too. You're a very good sick person."

"I don't have anyone to play with," I said.

"Look," my mother said, "I don't want you to be a phony, but I also don't want you to turn into the Great Complainer. Let's consider this period in your life a time of reflection. You can review your good times in New Jersey. You can think pleasantly of good times to come, when you meet new friends at school, when the house is finished and you get to see Nancy every day. This is a time when you can get to know yourself better. Just who is Mildred Murphy? Do you like her? Can you pass the time with just Mildred Murphy for company? This is your time to find out. Not everyone has this chance. Sometimes living gets too busy. Some people never take time to think, to know themselves."

"Do you like yourself?"

My mother laughed. "Oh, I'm o.k. I guess. Oh sure, I'm great! Don't ask me things like that!"

"What do you think about when you think?" I said.

"I think how lucky I am to have such a nice family. Really! I've always been lucky. I have nice parents and a nice brother."

"We both have a brother," I said. "That's sort of interesting and probably unusual."

"I think about the important thing I'm going to do in my life," she said.

"What are you going to do important?" I asked.

"I don't know. It's going to be something. I'm sort of waiting for the time to do it. I don't even know what it is. I thought it might be a poem I had to write. But I wrote the poem one day, and I knew it wasn't that."

My mother smiled and felt my forehead with her fingertips.

"What was it about?"

"About a fight Daddy and I had, about how I wanted to leave. I wanted to fly away in a plane as far away as I could go."

"But you're afraid to fly."

"I know. That's what I wrote in the poem. I'm afraid to fly."

"You won't leave will you?" I asked. My stomach inside was all shaky.

"Oh no! I was only mad for ten minutes. It was only ten minutes of madness. I just wanted to get it down on paper. There must be millions of husbands and wives who get mad for ten minutes, and I thought I'd capture the feeling for them. I didn't."

"You won't get divorced?"

"Mildred! For heaven's sake. I love Daddy and he loves me. In every marriage there are a few ten minute fights. In every relationship. What do you think I thought when Pa-Pa and Nana sent me to my room for punishment when I was little?"

"Did you hate them?"

"You bet I did! I also vowed I would never leave my room. Ever. They'd have to scrape me out of it. Of course in about an hour I'd walk down the stairs I never thought I'd ever step on again. They would smile at me, and the love feeling would slip back into the house."

"What did you do that got you punished?"

"I don't remember. Now I think it might be something with my hands that I'll do."

"You draw nice cartoons," I said.

"Oh, not like that. I want to make something beautiful. I think I might sculpt something, someday. Like a swan. I think I might be able to mold with my hands a beautiful curving swan, one that could take the outdoors, like a stone swan, on a patio."

"Would you sell it?"

"I might. If I can make one. I don't know." She touched my neck. "Your glands are swollen. No wonder you can't move your head."

My mother has on black and white checked slacks today and a yellow sleeveless polo shirt. She's more interesting looking than pretty. Allison used to say her mother was the prettiest person in the world. She wasn't, and I think it's a shame Allison didn't realize that. Her mother was even sort of ugly. My mother would have coffee with her about once a month. My mother said Allison's mother was her friend but she didn't want to see her every day. That was hard for me to understand because I saw Allison every day. Once I said to my mother, "I'm sorry you're lonely," and she said, "I'm not lonely. I'm complete. I am comfortable with my family, with myself. I'm not in desperate need of others though I do find their company pleasant at times. I wouldn't think of confiding in anyone but you and Jason and Dad. You are my best friends."

I guess I'm not complete yet. I would like very much . . . desperately . . . to have someone to play with right now. Dear Diary, you are a good friend but you're just not real and you don't talk back. Still, I like you.

Love, Mildred

P.S. I can't believe I wrote so much with a stiff neck!
P.P.S. Do you think Gertie is mad at me because I didn't take her to the bus stop yesterday? I wouldn't want Gertie mad at me. I wonder how she likes being back in Detroit?

Friday, July 22, it's bedtime

 Dear Diary,

Sorry I haven't written in you for a couple of days. But today I am better and I was allowed to go outside.

I met Mrs. Houghton skipping rope. She wasn't skipping rope. That was me. She was trying to get by me on the sidewalk.

She is really tall. I bet she is six feet tall and she looks like you might picture a big but pleasant looking witch. She wears too much powder and rouge so that it's very noticeable. And she looks like a person that has lost weight but is still wearing her fat clothes. Her dress moved in waves around her and didn't give her very good balance.

"Pardon me, dear, may I pass by?" she said.

I turned around and there she was.

"Hi," I said. "I'm Mildred Murphy."

"How do you do, Miss Murphy," she said. "I am Alicia Houghton."

I'm afraid then I didn't say anything. People who drink too much can be very nice and polite. People that don't drink at all can become tongue-tied.

She went on into Mrs. Murchison's house. I didn't

know they knew each other. Maybe she is one of the people in Mrs. Murchison's people garden.

All morning I tried not to look at the garage. I didn't want to think about Gertie. But finally I couldn't resist. I sat down on our green steps, cupped my chin in my hands, and looked at the garage and thought about Gertie's blueberry pie and the day I first saw her in her pink-flowered hat sneaking between the roses. I thought about our cups of tea and our talks. I thought of how meeting Gertie had helped me from missing Allison and Jerry and Lynne so much. I thought so hard it actually seemed I could see her at the garage apartment window. I imagined that she was waving at me. I rubbed my eyes. "Mirages," I thought. I looked back at the garage. I still saw someone— Gertie?—waving at me. I scratched my head. I knew Gertie was in Detroit. She had been there about four days. Then who was in the garage apartment waving at me?

I crossed the street. The person was waving and eating an apple. It sure looked like the same size as—it just had to be—it *was* Gertie !

I walked under the bay tree. She opened the door and came out on the stairway.

"You're back," I said.

"I never left," Gertie said. "Remember, we didn't say goodbye. I couldn't go without saying goodbye to my Mildred. When you didn't come to take me to the bus station I knew something was wrong."

"I had an ear infection."

"So I phoned Janet. Told her I'd be delayed a few days till I saw you again."

"You're still here," I said. I couldn't believe it.

"Now I've seen you," Gertie said. "Now I'll have to go of course."

"Today?"

"Let's make it tomorrow," Gertie said. "We'll do something today. Go for a walk. Sail a kite. We'll have ourselves a day." When Gertie came down the stairs she said, "I'll show you some places I discovered these past few days."

"You've been exploring San Rafael?" I said.

"Oh, such a nice town. It's charming. I hate to leave."

We started walking toward town and turned onto Mission. I think they have the tallest palm trees in the world on Mission Avenue. We passed several mansion-type homes. We came to the beginning of a long driveway. A sign said B.P.O.E.

"It's the Elks Club," Gertie said. She started to walk up the long drive.

I hesitated.

"My Everett was an Elk," Gertie said. "It's all right."

There was so much greenery everywhere. Then we walked through a tall hedge to a place of statues and white benches.

"It's a formal garden," Gertie said.

Before I came to California I thought a garden had cornstalks and tomato plants. But now I knew about Old Man Porter's lemon trees, the Calloway's rose garden, my mother's attempt with marigolds, Mrs.

Murchison's people garden, and now this Elk's club formal garden.

"The big house was a mansion. There's a swimming pool on the upper level. This is for garden parties." Gertie put her arms out and turned around. "How about an outdoor wedding here? Wouldn't it be something?"

We sat on a bench. The garden did feel partyish and grand. I pretended I was a princess.

"You know, there's something wonderful about the Elks," Gertie said. "They never forget old friends that are gone. Every night at eleven o'clock they stop whatever they are doing; they pause to remember the old friends that are gone. Back in Detroit they think of Ev every night."

I got up and walked around the fountain in the middle of the garden. Red and pink flowers were planted at the base. I felt like rolling in the grass but I wasn't sure a princess would do that. I started skipping across the garden.

Gertie was smiling, there on the bench. "Look at the magnolia trees," she said.

"I love flowers," I said, running to the ones in the middle of the garden. I ran back to Gertie and I hugged her. "And I love people," I said. "I think when I grow up I will have a garden like this with both plants and people. It will be a gentle garden. I'll be careful not to step on the flowers or on people's feelings. There will be birds singing in the trees and also bees and grasshoppers. The people will be so happy. They won't be allowed to get old or poor or lonely. It will always be summertime. It will be a summertime garden."

"You're describing California," Gertie said. "California is a summertime garden."

After awhile Gertie said why didn't we go to another place she had found. She took two apples out of her purse and gave one to me. We had to walk through town. On C Street I ran up to a girl walking by and almost knocked her down.

"I'm sorry," I said. "I thought you were somebody from New Jersey."

I walked back to Gertie. "I feel so stupid. I thought it was Marcelline Goodman. I would have bet a million dollars it was Marcelline."

Gertie patted my back. "I've done that. A lot of people in this world must look alike. Maybe we all have secret twins."

"If I see Allison's twin here in California, I'll die!" I said.

"We still have a way to go," Gertie said, picking up the pace.

"Allison writes me the dumbest letters. You wouldn't believe them. They don't say anything. When I write to her I write pages and pages but all she says is how are you? how is your mother? how is your father?"

"Aha! It's this way," Gertie said. She took my hand.

"Gertie, what would you do about Allison if you were me?"

"Mildred, what do you want to do about Allison?"

"I don't know. I guess I'll never see her again," I said. It was the first time I had admitted that.

"Probably not," Gertie said.

"I think she'll stop writing to me. She doesn't have anything to say."

"That happens," Gertie said.

"Well I won't stop writing to her until she stops writing to me," I said. "I'm going to write pages and pages and pages to her. But if she ever stops writing to me . . ."

"Here we are!" Gertie said. "It's the Louise A. Boyd Museum."

There are all kinds of animal exhibits at the Louise A. Boyd Museum. Stuffed animals and scorpions and things to learn about. And they give nature walks. I'm glad Gertie found it for me.

My last day with Gertie Wilson was nice. When we got back we made plans for going to the bus stop in the morning. I better not get sick this time, Gertie says! And Gertie told me she would always write to me and never stop. She said she would write about what she was doing and what her grandchildren were doing. The postal workers between San Rafael and Detroit are really going to be busy.

Love, Mildred

P.S. My mom just called up to me. "Bring down your dirty clothes," she said. "I haven't seen any dirty clothes from you for a week. What are you doing with them, eating them?" I'm so tired. I'll take down my dirty clothes tomorrow.

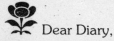 Dear Diary,

Here is what happened as well as I can figure out. Part of it I know happened because I was there, unfortunately! Part of it I figured out myself. I was sleeping. I guess Mother had had it with me and my dirty clothes. She came up to get them herself and probably muttered something like, "Can you tell me why a child puts dirty clothes piled into the drawers with clean clothes?" Then I guess she grabbed a bundle of dirty underwear, scooping you, dear diary, out with it, and on the stairs you fell out and bounced down the steps and flew open at the bottom to a very interesting page.

It must have been the page where I said Mother was a loner because she keeps stressing to me that she only read the parts involving Gertie. Then she'll say, "And Mildred, I am *not* a loner. I am merely selective with my friendships."

Anyhow, she and Dad read about Gertie Wilson living in the Calloway garage apartment without the Calloways knowing it. They dragged me out of bed at eleven o'clock at night, and we all went over to the Calloways. I was in my red bathrobe.

Dan and Irene couldn't believe what my mother was telling them. She had to say it several times. I had to

71 ❦

tell them too. Finally they believed us. We all walked out to the garage, and Dan and my dad went up to the garage apartment.

Poor Gertie. Dad said she had been sleeping, and she got all embarrassed. Then my dad and Dan came out of the garage while Gertie got dressed. We stood around looking at each other, waiting for Gertie. Dan kept moving his chin. My mother looked like she had a fever of 104.

Gertie didn't come and didn't come. Everyone was getting impatient. Dan went up the stairs and knocked on the apartment door again. It was quiet for a long time. Then we heard Gertie call, "Be there in a second."

But then she didn't come and didn't come again. Dan had a perturbed look on his face. I couldn't imagine what was taking Gertie so long. Then I had a terrible thought. Maybe she was doing something desperate. When the adults weren't looking I walked away. Everything seemed all right at the front of the garage. Then I walked around to the other side of the garage. It was probably the worst side, termite-wise. It was the side of the apartment that had the sagging floor. I looked up and saw Gertie hanging there like a Mary Poppins floating down from the sky.

"Oh Mildred, good, you're here," she said. "My foot is stuck."

She was about eight feet off the ground.

"What are you hanging on?" I said.

"It's my clothes. See, here's my blue blouse. I tied all my clothes together. Then I fastened them to a

piece of clothesline hanging from the roof beam, threw the clothes out the window and now I'm climbing down."

"Couldn't you have tied sheets together?" I asked.

"Yes, if I had some. Only have my clothes. Ooff," she puffed, struggling to free her foot while she banged back and forth against the wall of the garage.

All of a sudden there was a sickening crack. That was when the garage roof caved in. Gertie tumbled to the ground. It wasn't far and I guess she's pretty spry because she stood right up, kind of shaky but still up. About two seconds later our side of the garage started swaying. The window broke. I heard my mother scream. My father was yelling my name. Our side of the garage stopped swaying and sort of leaned into its middle. I knew I had to let my parents know I was all right. But I had to know what Gertie was going to do.

"You can run away if you want, Gertie. I have to let my mother know I'm not hurt." I grabbed Gertie and kissed her then I ran to my parents.

"Here I am," I said. "Mrs. Wilson is all right too. But she has decided to leave. She got out through the window on the other side of the garage."

Dan ran from his house. "The rescue squad and fire department are coming!" he called.

"Mrs. Wilson got out, Dan. She's all right," Irene said. "She's also gone."

"You mean I called the rescue squad for nothing?" Dan said.

"Perhaps they could rescue my clothes," a soft voice

said. Then Gertie came into view. She smiled sort of funny at me. She was wobbly-kneed. I ran to her. I hugged her.

"Mom and Dad," I said. "This is Gertie. My friend."

The fire trucks and rescue squad arrived. A newspaper reporter came too, and took pictures. The firemen disconnected the electricity and got Gertie's clothes. Dan assured them the garage would be torn down tomorrow. Gertie, Mom and Dad and I went in the Calloway's house.

Irene suggested Dan make drinks for the grown-ups. He made a double for himself. I could understand that. I wished I had a double Dr. Pepper.

Gertie began to talk. She explained that Irene's mother had asked her to come to California to live in the garage apartment, how she was shocked to learn her friend had died, how out of desperation she took up residence in the garage apartment without telling Dan and Irene. She apologized and begged them to forgive her.

Everybody did although it took Dan longer than anyone else. In fact they made a real fuss over Gertie. I was completely ignored.

Gertie explained that she would be flying to Detroit, that she would have been there already if I hadn't gotten sick. Irene insisted she sleep the night in their house. My mother and father wanted her to stay with us. Gertie didn't know what she should do! And I wished I had told my parents about her a long time ago, the first day I saw her through the telescope.

There was a knock on the door. It was Old Man Porter and Mrs. Murchison. They had seen all the lights on at the garage and the rescue squad and fire trucks and wondered what was going on. Well, Old Man Porter wondered. Mrs. Murchison *knew.*

"Hello everyone," Mrs. Murchison said, smiling happily. "I came to ask the lady if she would like to live at my house for a few weeks. I want to give her time to decide her future. I think the two of us, being in the same age bracket, would get along."

"But how do you know about Gertie?" I asked.

"I don't know all the details. But I know enough. In every neighborhood there is one person who generally makes it her business to know what is going on. *I* am that person," Mrs. Murchison said.

"I thought *I* was that person," Old Man Porter said. "But I don't know a blamed thing."

Everyone laughed and Irene filled Porter in on the details about Gertie while Dan filled everyone's glass again. Mrs. Murchison took Gertie aside and talked with her. As much as I wanted Gertie to stay with us I sort of expected her to choose Mrs. Murchison, since she's an expert on people and I'm only just a beginner. I was right. Gertie decided to live at Mrs. Murchison's for a few weeks to think some more about finding a job she would get paid for or going back to Detroit and into a retirement home.

Well, I don't know what I'm so gloomy about. She'll be right next door! Boy, am I sleepy.

Mildred

As soon as I woke up this morning I looked out the window at the smashed Calloway garage. There were two men loading its broken boards on a big truck and carting it away. Something was all over. I wasn't sure what. All of a sudden I wanted to see my mother very badly. I ran downstairs and found her in the backyard planting marigolds and snail pellets. She opened her arms and I ran into them.

"Oh Mommy," I cried.

"Mildred, what's wrong?"

"If something happens to Gramps or Grannie, or Pa-Pa or Nana, what will we do?"

She patted my head. "I don't know, honey. I just don't know."

"Will the one that's left come to live with us?"

"I don't know," she said, softly. "Sometimes a house just isn't big enough to have two sets of people living in it."

"What's the answer then?"

"I don't know the answer, Mildred. I don't think anyone knows the answer."

We watered the marigolds together and somehow it made me feel better.

My mother said, "It's difficult to know what to do

when people grow older, to know what responsibilities you as their child should have. Some people believe that because they raised you as a child, you are responsible to bring them into your home and care for them when they are too old to care for themselves. I'm not sure where I stand. I'd hate to have to put Pa-Pa or Nana in a nursing home if it made them unhappy. If they would cry about it, it would kill me. But I'm not so sure you or Jason or Daddy should have to live in a house with a very old person where you had to be oh so quiet and oh so careful not to hurt their feelings. And you would have so little left of me because I would be devoting so much time to them. Perhaps I would be cross from tiredness. At any rate, Mildred, you will have no such worry with me. We'll make things clear right now. I do not expect or want you or Jason to take care of me when I am old. Put me in a retirement home or nursing home, whatever is necessary.''

"But what if you're lonely?" I asked.

"I assure you I will be happy," Mother said.

"But what if you're scared?" I said.

"I know a secret, Mildred. You can be happy anywhere *if* you want to be. And I do.''

"But what if you're old and lonely and scared and you shake?" I said.

Mom hugged me. "Oh honey, it does happen, doesn't it? Doesn't it? Well, if it happens to me I'll try to remember how sweet and caring and loving you are right this moment. I'll try to remember and not be scared.''

Mom said we should pick a few marigolds to put on the kitchen table.

"I know you're worried about Mrs. Wilson," she said. "You've been a very good friend to her, Mildred. You cared for her and helped her when she was lonely and confused. You make me realize how important friends are. Maybe I should reach out more. But don't worry that Mrs. Wilson has been discovered. Now that the whole town knows the problem there will be more ideas on how to solve it."

To prove her point she showed me the morning paper. There was a front page article about the whole Gertie story, with pictures. And I'm in my bathrobe! On the editorial page there was a really interesting article about when people get old and how it's hard for them to have enough money to eat and live and everything. It says the paper will soon run a series of articles for senior citizens. Topics like "How To Cope On A Fixed Income," "Nutrition Programs Subsidized By The State" and "How To Apply For Medical Assistance, Free Hunting And Fishing Licenses, Reduced Rates On Buses." Things like that.

Being old is hard to imagine when you are ten. But I will be old someday. I wonder if I will want to fish and hunt then? I went out on the front porch steps to think about it. I guess I had my head resting on my hands and a frown on my face because Milly came by with a peach colored throw rug on her arm and asked why I was looking so mean.

"I always look mean when I'm thinking," I said.

"Must be something serious," she said, sitting down beside me.

"Have you heard about Gertie Wilson?" I said.

"Uh-huh. Mrs. Johnson showed me your picture in the paper and told me all about it. You're a superstar, Nosie."

"Well, what do you think about Gertie?"

"My, that's a problem all right. People get old nobody wants them. I'm lucky I got the Johnson's. I know old people who are so poor and alone they sleep in till noon so they don't have to eat breakfast—can't afford it. They practically sleep their life away. Then when they die they can't afford to be buried."

"I get sick thinking about it."

"Well, what can she do?" Milly said.

"The only thing she can do is cook and bake and babysit," I said.

"Well that's something," Milly said. "She can start from there."

"I don't think she can earn enough babysitting."

"With you to spread the word? With old Nosie out there pounding the sidewalk drumming up business for her friend, Mrs. Wilson?" Milly paused and laughed. "She'll be a babysitting tycoon before she knows it!"

I looked at Milly. And suddenly I saw myself passing out leaflets and telling the whole neighborhood, the whole town, that they should use Gertie as their babysitter.

"Milly, do you think I can do it? I mean do you really think I can?"

"I have faith in my superstar," Milly said. Then she stood up and shook the peach colored rug.

"Hey Milly," I said, remembering something. "Gertie was my secret. You know my secret now."

Milly stopped shaking the rug and looked at me. "That's right," she said. "I do."

"But I don't know yours."

Milly shook and shook that peach colored rug. She about shook it to death.

"You know mine," I reminded her.

"Oh, tut, mine's nothing special," Milly said, kind of muttering. "Just because a body can't read or write. Just because I never got to go to school. No reason to keep that old secret anymore." She started to leave then she turned back and said, *Only don't you tell a soul!*"

I went over then to Mrs. Murchison's to see Gertie. But nobody answered the door.

As I stepped back on our front porch I saw an ambulance stop up in the next block. The men in the white suits lifted someone into the house. I suppose Mrs. Murchison will know all about it. Or will she? Nancy phoned me this afternoon to say she was sorry for telling her great-aunt my secret. That's how she knew.

I'm not very good at keeping secrets either. At dinner I told Mother and Dad about Milly not knowing how to read or write.

I wonder where Gertie and Mrs. Murchison were today?

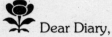 Dear Diary,

I saw Gertie today. I went over to Mrs. Murchison's house and knocked on the door. Gertie answered it. She had on her yellow dress. She smiled and hugged me.

"Does my dress look all right? You can't imagine how wrinkled all my clothes were!"

"It looks fine. How have you been?" I asked.

"Grace Murchison and Al Porter showed me San Francisco yesterday!"

I smiled. "You're making new friends too," I said.

"Come see my room."

It was on the first floor. It used to be a den. It looked real nice. It had green and white wallpaper. There was a twin bed covered with a white quilt with red and green dolls holding hands in a circle. She had a chest of drawers that matched the bed and a comfortable green chair. There were three geraniums on her windowsill. She said Irene Calloway brought her the geraniums. I looked out her window.

"Hey! There's our backyard! I can wave to you." Gertie smiled.

"This room is *nice*," I said. "It's much better than a termite garage, don't you think?"

Gertie looked thoughtful. "Did all that really happen? It seems like a dream. I don't know what possessed me. Sometimes we do things we never in this world thought we would do."

"Will you stay here?"

Gertie looked at the red geraniums. "I'll stay for awhile," she said. "For the time it takes to think. Assemble my life. Grace says anything is possible. Just think positive! Well, I don't want to bother you about it. How about a cup of tea?" She clapped her hands and stood up.

"Gertie, do you know what I want for you? At the end of each day when you take Everett's picture out from under your pillow I want you to be able to say 'I'm doing fine, Everett. I'm doing just fine today.' We have to think of the important things. You don't have much money but you have your health. And you have friends here and a family in Detroit that loves you. Gertie, I have lots of plans for you," I said.

"Well, come to the kitchen and let's hear them," she said. "I want to make a pot of tea."

We drank our tea and ate some lemon cookies Gertie made earlier when Old Man Porter had brought her ten big lemons from his trees. She liked my ideas about advertising her for babysitting and making cookies and cakes to sell.

"You know there's a nice bakery downtown. Maybe I could get a job. They can't discriminate about my age especially if I tell them I'm forty and Julia Child's estranged twin sister!" She laughed.

"Just take some samples. They won't be able to resist your lemon cookies and blueberry pie," I said.

"Whatever I decide to do I'll have to save enough money to pay for my room here and then enough to take the bus to Detroit for a Christmas visit. Won't that be something?" she asked.

"We'll make out a budget. I know you can do it, Gertie."

She looked wistful. "Maybe someday, my own apartment. I don't want to overstay my welcome here. I'm going to try to keep out of the way. I'll mostly stay in my room. I don't want Grace to be sorry she let me stay here."

"My dad saw an advertisement in the paper today for being someone's companion. You could do that. There are lots of things you could do. You just have to decide."

"You about take my breath away, Mildred."

I bit into my seventh lemon cookie. "Gertie, I know one thing. You are going to have to face the fact that you are the best babysitter and dessert-maker in Marin County, and I'm going to see that everyone finds out about it."

Gertie laughed. "I can almost feel myself on the bus to Detroit. I can almost see my darling grandchildren around the Christmas tree."

"Then you think you'll stay in California? You won't fly off to a retirement home?"

"I'm not absolutely sure," Gertie said, "but I think I ought to give California a try!"

"Hoo-ray!" I said.

So, this afternoon I drew up some leaflets advertising Gertie and I passed out forty-one, which is ten sore fingers worth. Mom said Dad will xerox more for me. I can't wait till people start phoning Gertie for babysitting and cookie orders!

When I went up in the next block and passed out a leaflet to Mrs. McWhirter she said it was good news because her daughter, Josie, had come home from camp with a broken leg from falling off a horse. (The ambulance I saw.) Mrs. McWhirter said she would certainly be using Gertie so she could get out shopping, etc. She invited me to come play with Josie. I said I had to deliver leaflets but I could come tomorrow. I wonder what Josie is like? Diary, I can't wait for tomorrow!

Love, Mildred

P.S. I was in bed and practically asleep. My mother came in and tapped me on the shoulder. She smiled and told me something special.

"Mildred, I've discovered the important thing I'm going to do in my life. I'm going to teach Milly to read and write. I guess I can mold a swan some other day."

"Does Milly know?" I asked.

"Yes. We had quite a talk this evening. Do you know she was trying to teach herself, by copying words out of the newspaper. There is so much she wants to do. Write to her daughter, Desileen. Help if she can. Find out if Desileen knows about her brothers. There's so much catching up for Milly to do, so many reasons she needs to read and write."

"When are you going to mold your swan?" I teased.

Mom laughed. "You can always mold a swan. You can wake up some day and say 'I'm going to mold a swan today' but sometimes you only get one chance in life to help another person."

"I love you, Mom," I said.

She kissed me on the end of my nose. She's silly and nice.

Love again, Mildred

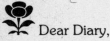 Dear Diary,

I went up to meet Josie McWhirter today. She is spoiled and hateful. But I like her o.k.

Of course I know Josie won't be as good a friend as Nancy. In fact I get the feeling Josie will drop me when school starts and she gets back in chummy with her old friends. But at least I know what she is like. Probably the type of person my mother wouldn't think would make a good friend. But we did have fun even though she was sometimes rude. And when school starts, Nancy will be there. So the drop won't be so hard.

I took you with me, diary, and told her she could read you if she wanted to know what had been going on in the neighborhood while she was at camp. She grabbed you greedily and read about five pages. Then she closed you WHAP and sort of tossed you aside.

"Your handwriting is so awkward and juvenile," she said. "I haven't written that way since I was in the first grade."

See what I mean about Josie? I bet the counselor at camp broke her leg.

But the visit wasn't all bad. She wanted me to teach her to blow her nose like Old Man Porter, and we had a great time doing that till her mother yelled at us. I told her a little about Gertie, and Josie says when she gets her walking cast she'll help me pass out leaflets. Her doctor is Happy too.

Then she told me Mildew wasn't a bad name but it was definitely a fourth grade name, and if I was going to go in the fifth grade, I'd have to have a good fifth grade name.

"What's a good fifth grade name?" I asked.

"Josie," she said.

"No kidding," I said.

"Of course, now that I'm going into sixth, I'll just be Jo this year."

"Well, what will *I* be?" I said.

She thought and thought. "Mia," she said. "Mia Murphy."

"Mia," I said. It sounded nice. I liked it! "Mia, Mia, Mia." I loved it!

So I autographed her cast. *Your friend, Mia Murphy.* And tomorrow after I pass out some samples of Gertie's cookies, I'm going to go up to Josie's and we're going to play.

You know, I sort of like it here in California!

Love, Mildred